D1294354

Spiders

Don McLeese

ROURKE
PUBLISHING
www.rourkepublishing.com

www.rourkepublishing.com

PHOTO CREDITS: Cover © Oleksiy Holubenko; Page Header © kontur-vid; Title Page © Fong Kam Yee; Table of Contents © Joanna Zopoth-Lipiejko; Page 4 © Cathy Keifer; Page 5 © Steve Collender , Matthew Field, http://www.photography.mattfield.com, Brian Chase, Meoita, D. Kucharski & K. Kucharska, Exactostock/Superstock; Page 6 © Giuliano C. Del Moretto; Page 7 © Morkelsker; Page 8/9 © Mirvav; Page 8 © Cathy Keifer; Page 10 © Cathy Keifer; Page 11 © Cathy Keifer; Page 12 © stocksnapp, ifong; Page 13 © Sebastian Kaulitzki, Arkady, Smit, Cosmin Manci; Page 14 © Ng Wei Keong; Page 15 © Péter Gudella; Page 16/17 © Cathy Keifer; Page 16 © Cathy Keifer; Page 18/19 © Dr. Morley Read; Page 18 © Cathy Keifer; Page 20 © Hugh Lansdown; Page 21 © Sanclemenesdigpro; Page 22 © LionH

Edited by Precious McKenzie

Cover Design by Renee Brady'
Layout by Nicola Stratford, Blue Door Publishing, FL

Library of Congress Cataloging-in-Publication Data

McLeese, Don
 Spiders / Don McLeese
  p. cm. -- (Eye to Eye With Animals)
 ISBN 978-1-61741-779-5 (hard cover) (alk. paper)
 ISBN 78-1-61741-981-2 (soft cover)
 Library of Congress Control Number: 2011924825

Rourke Publishing
Printed in the United States of America, North Mankato, Minnesota
091610
091510LP-B

ROURKE PUBLISHING

www.rourkepublishing.com - rourke@rourkepublishing.com
Post Office Box 643328 Vero Beach, Florida 32964

Table of Contents

Chapter 1

Creepy Crawlers!

Do spiders scare you? We know that spiders bite. We may even know that there is **poison** in their bite. So are we scared of spiders because they can hurt us?

Not really. In North America, there are only six kinds of spiders whose bite has **venom** that can hurt you. And world wide there are only 25 spiders who can hurt you with a bite.

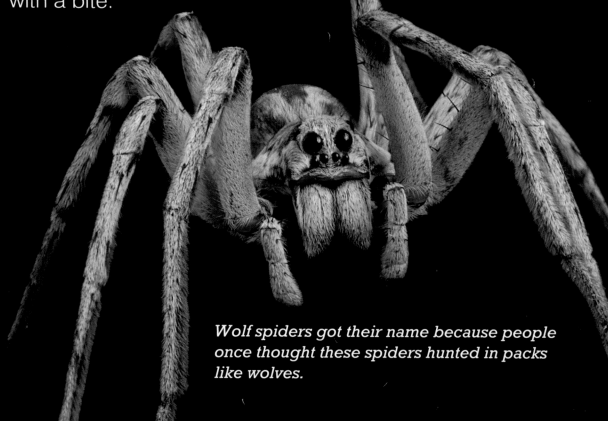

Wolf spiders got their name because people once thought these spiders hunted in packs like wolves.

You might think that's a lot of harmful spiders but scientists think there may be as many as 100,000 different kinds of spiders all over the world. They have already discovered and given names to more than 35,000 types, or **species**. There are billions and billions of spiders on Earth, so many that we couldn't begin to count.

North American Spiders that Are Harmful to Humans

Brown Recluse

Black Widow

Hobo Spider

Brown Widow

Yellow Sac Spider

Mouse Spider

Chapter 2

What Spiders Eat

People should be thankful for spiders. Spiders eat locusts, grasshoppers, and other insects that destroy plants. Spiders also eat insects that carry diseases, such as mosquitoes and flies.

Spiders trap much larger insects in their webs and then gobble them up. How's that for all natural pest control?

Argiope Spider

What else do spiders eat? There is a spider that lives in the **jungles** of South America that is more than ten inches (25.4 centimeters) wide. It is known as the goliath bird-eating spider. Other large spiders eat mice or small fish, even frogs. And spiders eat each other! Because female spiders are usually bigger and stronger than males, it's more common for females to eat males than the other way around.

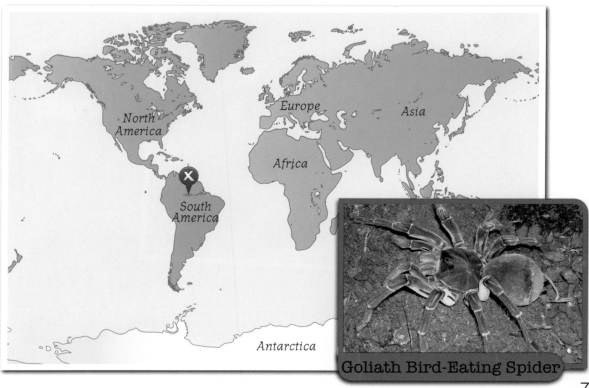

Goliath Bird-Eating Spider

Chapter 3
Hunters and Web Spinners

Since spiders don't eat plants, they have to capture **bugs** and other creatures for food. Some spiders go after their food and kill it. Other spiders, about half of all kinds, spin **webs** from sticky silk.

A female argiope spider wrapping silk around a grasshopper caught in her web.

Fascinating Spider Fact

The word "spider" comes from an Old English term that means to spin.

Argiope Spider

Spiders who spin webs usually can't see very well, so they eat the food that comes to them. Their webs are like sticky traps. Webs can be as wide as five feet across! (That's more than one and a half meters!)

Even spiders that don't spin webs can use silk to catch their food. Some use it like a cowboy's rope. Others shoot the sticky silk at their **prey**, which makes it hard for them to move or see.

▼ *Jumping spiders do not spin webs. Instead they secrete a silk tether that they use to jump from place to place.*

The wolf spider, unlike its terrifying name, helps people because it loves to dine on bothersome flies.

Chapter 4
Spiders and Insects

Most people think of spiders as a kind of **insect**, but they are not. Insects have six legs, and spiders have eight legs. Spiders belong to a group of animals known as **arachnids**.

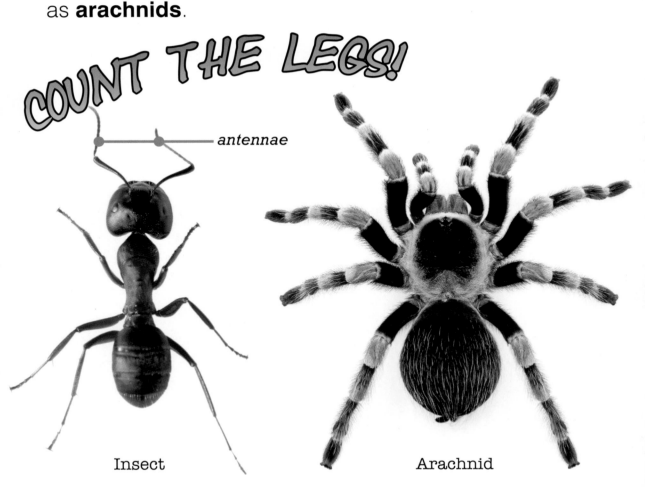

COUNT THE LEGS!

antennae

Insect

Arachnid

Many insects have wings, but arachnids don't. Other arachnids that are often confused with insects include scorpions and ticks.

Types of Arachnids

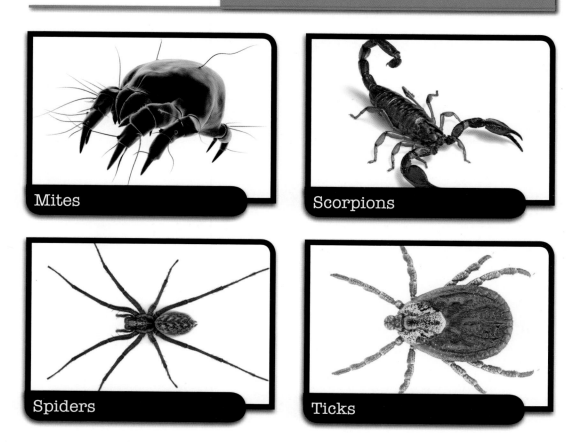

Mites

Scorpions

Spiders

Ticks

An insect's body has three parts, a head, thorax, and abdomen. But the spider's body has only two main sections. The spider's upper body combines the head and thorax (its chest) into a section called the **cephalothorax**. A shell called a carapace protects this section. The eight legs of the spider, in four sets of two, are attached to the cephalothorax. This section is also where the spider's eyes are.

cephalothorax

Jumping Spider

cephalothorax

Cross Spider

Many spiders have eight eyes, in four sets of two, just like their legs. Some have fewer. There are spiders that live in dark caves that have no eyes at all!

▲ *How many eyes does the female wolf spider have? If you counted eight, you are correct! All the better to see you with!*

A green lynx spider has eight eyes on top of its cephalothorax.

Spiders' **abdomens** have many important functions. They breathe through their abdomens. Their hearts are in their abdomens. And this is also where female spiders have their ovary, with eggs to make baby spiders. A female spider lays about 100 eggs at a time, but larger ones can lay more than 2,000!

▲ *Spiders spin a silk case to wrap their delicate eggs.*

Newly Hatched
Spiderlings

Although many spiders live less than a year, some live more than 20 years. Even though some spiders have short lives, scientists believe that spiders have been around for almost 400 million years!

Chapter 5

Spiders and People

There are far more spiders around us than we are ever likely to see. If you do see them in your garden, they are probably helping plants stay alive by killing insects that eat plants. Spiders themselves eat bugs, not plants.

Some people even like to keep spiders as pets! They can be very interesting to watch as they spin their webs or capture their prey. You don't have to do much to take care of them, as long as they have enough to eat.

▲▲ The huntsman spider lives in tropical regions of the world. They love to snack on caterpillars.

Some people claim tarantulas make excellent pets. They are quiet and they won't chew up your shoes or furniture!

Maybe people shouldn't be so scared of spiders after all. Most of them don't hurt us. Because they eat insects that destroy crops, they can help us! So the next time you see a spider, don't squash it. Instead, remember all the helpful things spiders do for people.

▼ *Wasp spiders catch and eat harmful wasps. That can help people stay safe!*

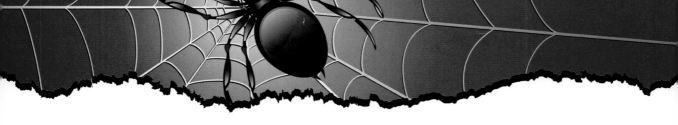

Glossary

abdomens (AB-duh-muhns): the rear part of a spider's body

arachnids (uh-RACK-nihds): bugs, like spiders, that have eight legs rather than six

bugs (BUHGS): small insects or insect-like animals

cephalothorax (SEFF-uh-low-THOR-aks): the front part of the spider, consisting of the head and the thorax

insect (IN-sekt): a small animal with six legs and no backbone

jungles (JUHNG-guhlz): tropical forests that are covered with trees, vines and plants

poison (POI-zuhn): something that can kill or harm an animal, person or plant when it is swallowed or sometimes even touched

prey (PRAY): an animal hunted for food by another animal

species (SPEE-seez): a group of animals or plants of the same kind

venom (VEN-uhm): a type of poison produced by some spiders and snakes

webs (WEBS): sticky nets of thin threads in which a spider catches insects to eat

Index

Websites To Visit

backyardnature.net/spiders.htm

cirrusimage.com/spider.htm

desertmuseum.org/books

About the Author

Don McLeese is a journalism professor at the University of Iowa. He has written many articles for newspapers and magazines and many books for young students as well.